William Bolcom

T0040844

Suite No. 1 in C minor
for Solo Violoncello

The **Suite No. 1 in C Minor** for solo violoncello is adapted from the score for the Arthur Miller play, *Broken Glass*, used in part in the Long Wharf (New Haven, Connecticut) and Booth (New York City) Theaters, in the Spring of 1994.

ISBN 0-634-07303-6

EDWARD B. MARKS MUSIC COMPANY

EXCLUSIVELY DISTRIBUTED BY

HAL•LEONARD® CORPORATION
7777 W. BLUEMOUND RD. P.O. BOX 13819 MILWAUKEE, WI 53213

For Norman Fischer
Jane Kenyon in memory

Suite No. 1 in C minor
for Solo Violoncello

DURATION: 17:00

WILLIAM BOLCOM
(1994-1995)

I. Prelude

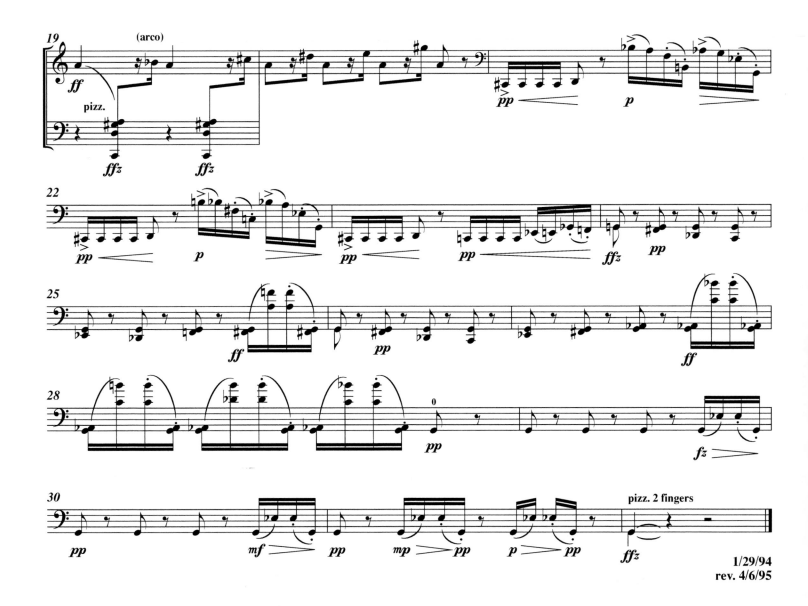

1/29/94
rev. 4/6/95

II. Arioso 1

1/30/94
rev. 4/6/95

𝄽 = a brief durational pause, slightly shorter than the traditional ,

III. Badinerie

2/7/94
rev. 4/6/95

IV. Arioso 2

4/7/95

This page left blank to avoid turns.

V. Alla sarabanda; tranquillo

9